T0082561

Making a Spiritual Connection

Connection

THROUGH
PRAYER, FASTING AND
MEDITATION—STUDY GUIDE

RALPH E. WILLIAMSON

authorHOUSE®

AuthorHouse™
1663 Liberty Drive
Bloomington, IN 47403
www.authorhouse.com
Phone: 1 (800) 839-8640

Published by AuthorHouse 03/07/2018

ISBN: 978-1-5462-2340-5 (sc)
ISBN: 978-1-5462-2339-9 (e)

Library of Congress Control Number: 2018900128

Print information available on the last page.

REW Ministries Logo (c) 2012
Manufactured and distributed by REW Ministries, Inc.

King James Version (KJV)
Public Domain

New King James Version (NKJV)
Scripture taken from the New King James Version®. Copyright © 1982 by Thomas Nelson. Used by permission. All rights reserved.

Contents

INTRODUCTION

Music is a powerful expression of worship. One of my favorite hymns of the church is, "I Am Thine O Lord."[1] The first lines of the third stanza captures my deep appreciation for the relationship I have with God. "O for a single hour before the throne I spend, as I commune with God as friend with friend." This hymn reminds me that God truly desires a personal relationship with each of us. This simple truth conceals a powerful principle - our need for God is matched, if not surpassed by His desire to be in relationship with us.

This book was developed from my experiences. Though I was raised in a Christian home, my spiritual journey earnestly began in adulthood. As I regularly prayed, meditated and fasted, I began growing spiritually and more importantly drawing closer to God. Later as a pastor, I observed many members who had joined the church and accepted Jesus Christ as their Lord and Savior. They were committed to the church, dedicated to their work and ministries, but struggled with their spiritual growth.

Many individuals had challenges with their prayer life; others understanding how to fast and apply

---

[1] Crosby, Frances Jane (1820-1915) "I Am Thine O Lord— [Draw Me Nearer]" Brightest and Best (New York: Biglow & Main, 1875), number 22. Music by W. Howard Doane.

spiritual discipline to transform their lives and renew their relationship with God. They were crying out from loneliness, depression, grief, financial and relational issues without relief. Gradually, I realized that they did not fully comprehend the fundamental spiritual disciplines of prayer, fasting, and meditation. I was convicted and compelled to seriously look at what I was doing wrong as a pastor, colleague, friend and indeed as a Christian.

After seeking the Lord for answers, I committed myself to sharing what God had taught me regarding spiritual development as it pertained to these disciplines. My fellow Christians, I will be so bold as to quote the Apostle Paul, *I have not obtained it all but one thing for sure, I keep pressing towards the mark of the high calling in Christ Jesus our Lord.* (Philippians 3:12) With this spirit of humility, I approached the task of learning and teaching. Through continuous prayer and the support of many who assisted in this project, I am able to present to you not just a study on spiritual disciplines; that effort has been done many times and created by those far better suited to the task. Instead, I offer a personal delineation of the ways I have practiced these disciplines over the years. This book was designed to help you develop a systematic spiritual approach to prayer, fasting and meditation. During this spiritual process using reflective reading and journaling you will obtain your desired outcomes.

The objectives of this book and its companion *Study Lessons* are to:

- Provide a framework to develop a personal strategy for enhancing your intimate relationship with God.
- Help you prepare for the fast, achieve your desire spiritual goals, and answers to your prayers
- Present spiritual instructions and specific study lessons as detailed in both the guide and companion book.
- Focus on six fasting goals for: The Individual, Family, Church, Community, World, Healing and Restoration.

The process outlined requires you to allow the Holy Spirit to lead and guide you with wisdom, knowledge and understanding. It is my prayer that this book enriches your spiritual growth and deepens your understanding of the power of these disciplines as you draw closer to God.

GETTING STARTED

Each day should be a time of spiritual renewal. As you look inwardly and take inventory of your life, you should ask the question, "What is missing"? One way to understand or determine what is missing in your life is to spend quality time with God while meditating and studying His Word. David understood this and sought God early in the morning. He prayed, meditated and communed with God, choosing to write when his body was rested and his mind was fresh. This quality connection and devotion is demonstrated when reading His words, *O God, you are my God; early will I seek You; My soul thirsts for you; My flesh longs for You in a dry and thirsty land.* (Psalm 63:1)

SPIRITUAL TRANSFORMATION
A PROCESS OF CHANGE

Quiet, intimate moments alone with God will transform your spiritual life. Do not be in a hurry when you are in the presence of the Lord. Spiritual transformation is a process of change that alters an individual's meaning, purpose, concerns and outcomes.

Take time to relax; free your mind from the anxiousness of the world, and allow your soul to connect with the spirit of God. As you listen to the voice of the

Lord speaking through the scriptures, you will actively develop your personal relationship with God.

God is not a creation of our imagination. He is not a thought or an idea. God is the source of all creation and the giver of life.

Without God, there is no air, water, light, darkness, meaning or purpose in the created order of the universe. And yet, more than anything else on earth, God desires to have an intimate relationship with us. God wants to be in relationship with you!

Not as an object of need or an afterthought; but out of love and compassion in hope that you will draw nearer to Him.

ALLOW GOD ACCESS

During your quiet moments alone, before making requests, celebrate His goodness, praise, and rejoice in His presence. Sit with God and in the presence of His love which encompasses your soul, rest in Him. Invite God to know your most treasured hopes, dreams and aspirations. Know that God is deeply interested in every aspect of your life. He has written, *Can a mother forget the baby at her breast And have no compassion on the child she has borne? Though she may forget, I will not forget you! See, I have engraved you on the palms of my hands; Your walls are ever before me.* (Isaiah 49:15-16)

God loves you! Trust Him to show you areas, places, events and people who will help in your transformation process. He needs you to allow His light and love to transform your life.

Search me, God, and know my heart; test me and know my anxious thoughts. See if there is any offensive way in me, and lead me in the way everlasting. (Psalm 139:23-24)

Once you allow God access to examine your life, the Divine Teacher will determine what you need to work on to develop an intimate prayer life. The Lord will meet you where you are. Communing with God through prayer is the foundation of your spiritual life. Your relationship to God will grow closer and the peace of God will surpass even your own understanding. When you stand in this space and place of divine connection you can tell God everything, your hurt, anxious desires, and celebrate your joys.

RELEASE, LET GO, LET GOD TAKE CHARGE

God has equipped you with everything you will ever need!

Through the anointing of the Spirit of God you have the ability to gain a higher spiritual dimension in understanding your meaning, purpose and fulfillment in life. Your greatest task in life is to become familiar with what God has given you. When reading the bible you will discover it is not simply a book of biblical laws, narratives, poems and miracles. It was inspired by God and is filled with the Holy Spirit for leading, guiding and directing our lives closer to God.

Each scripture is spiritually imbued with insight, revelations, wisdom, knowledge and understanding. You will discover life in the abundance and blessings are yours to receive! Trust the Lord, release, let go, let God take charge and He will bring the best out of you! I have prayed for you, and know that, *the author and finisher of our faith, who for the joy that was set before Him endured the cross, despising the shame, and has sat down at the right hand of the throne of God.* (Hebrews 12:2 KJV) When you allow the Lord to take charge, God will not permit you to do anything but succeed!

SPIRITUAL OBJECTIVE

The objectives of *Making a Spiritual connection through Prayer, Fasting, and Meditation* are threefold:

1. **Instruction** - Receiving spiritual instructions through the Word of God.
2. **Application** - How will you use what you have learned and apply it to your life, family, church, community and the world?
3. **Implementation** - Develop a personal strategy to accomplish your spiritual goals and desired outcomes. Summarize what you have learned.

CHAPTER 1

PRAYER

Call to me and I will answer you and tell you
great and unsearchable things you do not know.
(Jeremiah 33:3)

THE IMPORTANCE OF PRAYER

For the believer, living without prayer will put you in the spiritual Intensive Care Unit (ICU). In the ICU, a respirator breathes for the patient. This machine blows air into the lungs too weak to inhale air on their own. Reflexively, the lungs exhale. The movement of air in and out of the body causes the air to flow into the lungs; the heart is able to pump the blood and the body receives the nutrients for circulation and respiration. To the observer it appears as if the patient is breathing on their own. However, if the respirator is turned off, the lungs will not take in life-sustaining air. The heart will stop beating and the body will eventually die. Likewise, the Holy Spirit is our continuous respirator that keeps us connected to God through prayer. It is not one-sided but a two-way connection from the spirit of man to the spirit of God.

Prayer establishes two-way communication with God. The conscious choice to engage your spirit and stretch your consciousness from the limits of your body into the realm of the divine, connects you to our heavenly Father. You will connect with God when you lift your voice to Him who has ordained your existence. The One who loves you so much that He sent His only begotten Son; and the One who has your face graven on His palms and the hairs on your head numbered. In this place of intimacy, you receive strength as the Holy Spirit, changes and transforms you. This is why John McArthur explained that "For the Christians, prayer is like breathing."[2]

---

[2] (MacArthur 2006, 13)

Prayer sustains life. Because Satan understands very well what prayer means to a believer, your prayer life is always under attack! The enemy knows if he can cut off the source that enables you to live and communicate with God, it will weaken and eventually destroy your relationship with Him. Therefore, it should come as no surprise that our prayer life is the number one target of the enemy.

STAYING CONNECTED

We cannot live in this world without prayer. It is vital to everything you need to do and accomplish. Make no mistake if someone cuts off the constant flow of oxygen going into your lungs, your physical body will eventually die. The lungs would collapse first, your heart would stop working and your brain would no longer function. Likewise, your spiritual life will die without the constant flow of prayers. Our prayers flow from earth to heaven and from heaven to earth; from the spiritual man to the spirit of God. If you do not pray, you will find yourself in the spiritual ICU surviving off the prayers of others.

Many individuals are not aware, that they have someone standing in the gap connecting them to God. It could be your praying grandmother; your Sunday school teacher; your aunt who always reminded you that God loved you; your mother who never gave up crying out to God for your soul; the saints at the church you left; or the stranger at the grocery store who feels moved to say God bless you. Prayer is the source that gives life. In order to live, we must be connected to God through prayer.

- *Your spiritual life is connected to your relationship with God;*
- *Your relationship is connected to your salvation; and*
- *Your salvation is connected to your redemption that was brought and paid for by the blood of Jesus Christ.*

Prayer is a conscious action that aligns us with the Holy Spirit's power. When we turn to Jesus, His love connects us directly to God. It is Jesus who makes intercession for us so that our prayers will be answered. He is the one who stated everything we ask for, be it in God's will, will be "yes and amen." Jesus bridges the space between us and God giving us direct connection to God the Father. When we experience salvation, we become co-heirs with Jesus. We become the children of God. Jesus took on our sins so that we might be reconciled with God the Father. This is one of the reasons many people pray in the name of Jesus. This is to recognize and honor the connection that makes reconciliation with God the Father possible. When you pray, you activate, engage and develop this relational bond through Jesus with God. When you pray ask for direction, guidance, and wisdom of God to order your steps, change your situation, keep you from falling, protect you and save the lost. When you pray, begin to think, move and breathe with an openness to the directions of the Holy Spirit and a growing confidence in God's love.

A strong prayer life does not insulate you from problems, stress or disappointments. A strong prayer life prepares you for these challenges before they arrive and keeps you while you are going through. When you are attacked by doubt, buffeted by disappointments, lean into prayer. When you are at your wits end, when you can do no more, turn in faith and love to Jesus, who reminds us, *My grace is sufficient for you, for my power is made perfect in weakness.*[3] Do not allow the enemy, who seeks to destroy your relationship with God, trick you into turning away from prayer. When you are pressed on every side, when there seems to be no solution, when you have done all you can, leave room for the Holy Spirit. Your situation did not catch the Spirit of God by surprise.

When you give every thing to the Lord in prayer, you acknowledge His power over your life. Give your problems, challenges, situations, thoughts, wandering mind, foolish notions, and misguided energy to God. When you give everything to the Lord in prayer, you release control. When you release control you will no longer be like a ship tossed and driven by every wave and storm in life. In Hallesby's classic book on prayer, he wrote "He who gave us the privilege of prayer knows us very well. He knows our frame; He remembers that we are dust. That is why He designed prayer in such a way that the most impotent can make use of it. Prayer opens the door unto Jesus. And that requires no strength." [4] It is only a question of our will. Will you give Jesus access to your needs? It

[3] 2 Corinthians 12:9
[4] (Hallesby, Prayer 1994, 15)

seems counter-intuitive, to give away the very thing that gives you the power to change your situation. But when you acknowledge the lordship of Jesus, the power of the Holy Spirit and the love of God over every situation, the problems, even if they do not change in the ways you had hoped, it will give you a different spiritual perspective. No one solution fits every problem. But God, who knows you better than yourself knows what you need in order to be successful and at peace. His work is for eternity, not just for the present. Choose to believe His words, trust and learn to discern the movements of His hand in your life. God can and God will hear and answer your prayers.

THE INTIMACY OF A PRAYER LIFE

Mother Frances Dominica reminds us that, "Until we dwell in him and allow him to dwell in us, we shall be strangers." Prayer allows us to develop a relationship with God. We will never know God until we develop an intimate prayer life. You can know someone all of your life. You can see them, know something about them but not really know who they are, what they do, or what their motivations might be. You know them, but you do not have an intimate relationship. The intimacy of prayer is when nothing is withheld from God. *Draw near to God and He will draw near to you.*[5] The goal is to develop an intimate relationship with God. You will develop confidence in God as you learn more about who He is, what His promises are and just how much He loves you.

---

[5] James 4:8

In the process of drawing near to God by developing a relationship with Him, you will discover how awesome the love of God can be. His love reaches into every corner and dimension of our lives. It is so wide that it covers the breadth of our experiences; it is so long that it expands the length of our lives; it is so high that it rises to the heights of our celebrations. God's love is deep enough to reach the depths of discouragement, despair, even unto death. You will never be separated from the power of the love of God in Christ Jesus. You were designed to receive and respond to His divine love!

When you are in an intimate relationship with God, you will be changed. In spite of your circumstances you will be encouraged. Your perspectives on life, yourself and others will change. Other people will see your actions, responses, attitudes and even changes in your appearance. Whenever Moses was in the presence of God he was transformed. When he descended from the mountain and stood before the children of Israel, his face shined so brightly they could not look at him unless he wore a veil. (See Exodus 34:29-35) This was an external manifestation of an inner condition. The transforming love of God that takes place when we are in His presence!

PLACING OUR LIFE BEFORE GOD

Through honest, open dialogue of confessing and sharing intimate details of your life with the Lord, you will develop an intimate prayer life which will draw you closer to God. What does this look like? Paul explains in Romans,

So here's what I want you to do, God helping you: Take your everyday, ordinary life-your sleeping, eating, going-to-work, and walking-around, life-and place it before God as an offering. Embracing what God does for you. Don't become so well-adjusted to your culture that you fit into it without even thinking. Instead, fix your attention on God. Recognize what He wants from you and quickly respond to it.

Unlike the culture around you, always dragging you down to its level of immaturity, God brings the best out of you.[6]

A PRAYER OF COMMITMENT

It is human nature to make plans and then ask God to bless them. However, in every situation you should first seek God's will for your life. Whenever you choose to seek the Lord's will through prayer, you will gain insight into making the best decisions in every situation. Discerning and choosing to follow God's will for your life, will ultimately fulfill God's purpose for you. As you develop your relationship with God, you will hear His voice: *Your own ears will hear Him. Right behind you a voice will say, "This is the way you should go," whether to the right or to the left.*[7] EM Bounds writes in *The Necessity of Prayer* that "Nothing distinguishes the children of God so clearly and strongly as prayer,"[8] for prayer is the only

---

[6] Romans 12:1 MSG
[7] Isaiah 30:21 NLT
[8] (Bounds 2006, 62)

way in which the soul of man can enter into fellowship and communion with the giver of every good and perfect gift. Prayer enables you to discover and fulfill your divine destiny.

Each of us were uniquely created by God. Our needs and desires may be similar, but fulfillment is different for every individual. Likewise, our prayer life and how we pray is distinctly different. The events and circumstances in and around our lives will often dictate and influence how we pray. While there are helpful things we can learn in our approach to God, no one can tell you the right way to pray. If you are praying, you are already doing it right. God delights in hearing your prayers. But even more, God wants to have fellowship with you. Fellowship is the ultimate goal.

In Matthew 7:7, Jesus uses three verbs to describe prayer: ask, seek, and knock. Prayer is more than giving the Lord your requests. Prayer involves seeking His will to guide your life.

It means knocking on doors by exploring different solutions. Obtaining godly counsel to help in determining God's perfect and acceptable will for each situation in your life.

To know the will of God, you must first be willing to relinquish your own will. In the garden of Gethsemane, Jesus was faced with the awful reality of taking on the sins of the world, He cried out *remove this cup from me!* [9] Jesus was afraid, in pain and doubt. He was completely transparent with God about how he felt as he faced the

---

[9] Luke 22:42 KJV

cross. Jesus in his humanity turned to God in His deepest distress. God answered Him. Led by the Spirit, Jesus let go of His will and said, *Not my will, but yours, be done.* In the garden, the situation did not change. Jesus trusted God and in submission Jesus changed. Whenever you allow the will of God to take charge, the power of His Spirit will be released into your life.

Prayer is a simple act of communicating with God and surrendering your life to His will. Yet, we make it complicated by trying to manipulate and control the outcome. "We are to pray. God Himself will take care of the hearing and the fulfillment. He needs no help from us….The more of an effort prayer becomes, the more easily it is neglected."[10] Simply, ask, seek, knock and listen until you have clearly heard from the Lord. Then, put into action what you have heard and received.

ORGANIZING YOUR PRAYER LIFE

1. Establish a daily schedule. A consistent prayer life will give the greatest rewards.
2. Identify a sacred space where you and God will meet. This space is where your spiritual battles will be fought and victories won. *But when you pray, go into your room, close the door and pray to your Father, who is unseen. Then your Father, who sees what is done in secret, will reward you.*[11]

---

[10] (Hallesby, Prayer 1994)
[11] Matthew 6:6 NLT

3. Look for and choose a scripture to help focus your prayers while inviting the Holy Spirit into this sacred moment.

   And the Holy Spirit helps us in our weakness. For example, we don't know what God wants us to pray for. But the Holy Spirit prays for us with groanings that cannot be expressed in words. And the Father who knows all hearts knows what the Spirit is saying, for the Spirit pleads for us believers in harmony with God's own will.[12]

4. Be intentional with your time. Organize and identify who and what you are praying for. A great way to do this is to use specific days of the week to focus on:

• Personal prayer requests
• Family needs and concerns
• Requests from others
• Church
• Community
• World problems
• Leaders in all forms of government

5. Keep a journal regarding your prayer requests.

• Write down the date and time you began your petition.
• What is the specific request?

---

[12] Romans 8:26-27 NLT

- Be patient, wait on the Lord and remain consistent with the request until you are sure you have heard from the Lord.
- Record the date and time your prayer is answered.
- Celebrate your victory with praise and thanksgiving.

Finally, prayer is an organic connection between you and God. Activate the power of prayer. *Pray without ceasing,*[13] and watch what amazing things God will do.

> *Prayer:*
>
> *Lord Jesus, today, I present my body, mind and soul to you. I invite you to come into every aspect of my life. As I prepare for the challenges before me, your words are my source of hope and inspiration. I meditate on your Word both day and night. Each step I take, I take in faith.*
>
> *Your spirit lives and dwells within me. As I look at my family and friends I will see your grace. As I enter my work place, I bring your peace with me. As I drive, walk and interact with strangers, I will see your reflection. I will trust that you are working all things out for my good. Therefore, no matter what happens today, I will not be overwhelmed. I will not forget to help someone along the way. Bless your name Lord! Amen.*

---

[13] Thessalonians 5:16-18 KJV)

PRAYER WALKING

*One of the most rewarding and meaningful
walks is a prayer walk with the Lord.
It will enhance your spiritual life
beyond anything you can imagine!*

PRAYER WALKING

Go and walk through the land in every
direction, for I am giving it to you.
(Genesis 13:17)

In addition to your quiet time in the comfort of your home, office, or whatever spiritual place you have designated to be alone with God, you are encouraged to include a prayer walk as a part of your weekly, if not daily, meditation. Prayer walking is beneficial physically and spiritually. It is a time for you to maintain a healthy physical body and to communicate with God. One of the greatest examples of the ultimate reward of walking and having a conversation with God is recorded in the biblical story of Enoch. *Enoch walked with God; and then he was no more, because God took him away.*[14]

> Godliness is walking with God: which shows reconciliation to God, for two cannot walk together except they be agreed. [1.] Walking with God pleases God. [2.] We cannot walk with God so as to please him, but by faith. [3.] God himself will put an honor upon those that by faith walk with him so as to please him. He will own them now, and witness

---

[14] Genesis 5:24 NLT

for them before angels and men at the great day.[15]

As you are walking and meditating on the Word, God wants to hear from you. Ask the Lord to open your eyes and order your steps. You cannot bring your potentiality into actuality without an inner drive to understand who you are. You are not just here to occupy space. Every facet of your life is relevant to why the Lord created you. *The Lord spoke to Moses and declared; I have raised you up for this very purpose, that I might show you my power and that my name might be proclaimed in all the earth.* (Exodus 9:16)

- When Jeremiah was called, it was the Lord that spoke to him and said: *Before I formed you in the womb I knew you; before you were born I sanctified you.* (Jeremiah 1:5 NKJV)
- Mordecai sent this message to *Esther, Do not think that because you are in the king's house you alone of all the Jews will escape. For if you remain silent at this time, relief and deliverance for the Jews will arise from another place, but you and your father's family will perish. And who knows but that you have come to your royal position for such a time as this?* (Esther 4:13-14)
- *Many are the plans in a person's heart, but it is the Lord's purpose that prevails.* (Proverbs 19:21)

---

[15] (Bible Hub 2016)

Many individuals never get beyond the self-discovery stage which limits their ability to achieve their greatest spiritual potential and purpose. God alone knows the plans for our lives. Therefore, we must seek spiritual guidance and direction. Walking, meditating and talking with God is an excellent opportunity for the Lord to reveal secrets. As our awareness is enhanced, we will discover an untapped potential waiting to be used. Whenever you commit to moving beyond the narrow limitations of your personal ambitions and desires, your entire outlook on life will change. In your walk, choose to dedicate or recommit your life, surrender to the Lord and let God have His way!

REMAIN FOCUSED

Many years ago as a new Christian I discovered the power of prayer walking while trying to resolve a spiritual issue about baptism. This took place during my years working as a letter carrier in the US Postal Service. I decided to use my time wisely. Instead of just walking alone and delivering mail in the city of Colorado Springs, I declared a fast. For three days, I prayed and walked all day meditating on the Word of God while delivering the mail. This was my first experience with fasting, praying, and walking with a spiritual purpose. On the third day I completed my fast and finished my prayer walk. Most importantly, God gave me the answer.

Remember to use your time wisely with the Lord. The prayer walk should be intentional and focused. Raise your concerns.

Your concerns are God's concerns. No matter what you are going through, God is not through with you. Make room during your walk to be attentive to the movements of God in your life.

Suggestions to help you maintain your focus:

- Prepare your heart with scripture to meditate upon.
- Reflect and take notice of your surroundings (people, places and things) and how they relate to your current situation.
- Make intercessory prayer for others as the spirit leads you.
- Yield and be open to the Lord's calling and purpose.

Chapter 2

FASTING

Fasting is more than a diet adjustment. It is a spiritual discipline that involves spiritual agony which leads to a deeper understanding of the will of God and spiritual growth.

FASTING

*I proclaimed a fast… that we might humble
ourselves before our God to seek from
Him the right way for us.*
(Ezra 8:21)

You may face many challenges, difficulties, and
problems. Challenges are not limited to only what
you and your family might experience. Our church,
community and world are being negatively impacted.
Therefore, it is imperative to seek divine guidance for
strategies and solutions to various problems. In addition
to prayer, fasting is a constructive way to truly connect
with God while dealing with our individual and collective
challenges. *Commit your way to the Lord, Trust in Him,
and He shall bring it to pass. He shall bring forth your
righteousness as the light, And your justice as the noonday.*
(Psalm 37:5-6 NKJV)

This spiritual discipline was purposefully designed
for individuals to make a sacrifice with the expectation
of hope and anticipation for something new to occur.
Fasting is more than a diet adjustment. It is a spiritual
discipline that involves spiritual agony which leads to a
deeper understanding of the will of God and spiritual
growth. It is widely practiced in both the Old and New
Testament and commonly used by individuals from
all walks of life. For example, in the Old Testament, it
was extremely important for the entire community to
demonstrate their mutual support in time of difficulty.

In the biblical context as written by Elmer L. Towns, *Fasting for Spiritual Breakthroughs:*

> Fasting apparently began as a natural expression of grief. After time it became customary to prove one's grief to others by abstaining from food. David fasted to demonstrate his grief at Abner's death. (2 Samuel 3:35).
>
> Many references in scripture describe fasting as "afflicting" one's soul or body. (Isaiah 58:3,5). Fasting came to be practiced as an external means of demonstrating and later encouraging an internal feeling of remorse for sin. Fasting was a perfectly natural human expression of human grief; therefore, it became a religious custom to placate the anger of God. People began fasting to turn away God's anger from destroying them. Eventually, fasting became a basis for making one's petition effective to God. David defended his fasting before the death of his son by Bathsheba, indicating his hope that while the child lived David's prayer might be answered. When the child died, David promptly ended his fast denoting that he knew then that neither fasting and praying could any longer avail. (2 Samuel 12:15-23)[16]

Spiritual growth should always be the desired outcome of any fast. A meaningful fast must be godly inspired and directed. If our fasting is not unto God, there can be no spiritual breakthrough, growth, or development.

---

[16] (Towns 1982, 25-26)

PURPOSE

Is not this the kind of fasting I have chosen: to loose the chains of injustice and untie the cords of the yoke, to set the oppressed free and break every yoke? (Isaiah 58:6)

Before starting a fast clearly state what you want to accomplish. There should be a specific purpose.

1. Fasting begins with prayer and the Word of God. This is the structure of every successful fast: prayer, the Word and you.
2. Pray a prayer of consecration and dedication as you share with God the reason you are embarking on the fast.
3. Before you start fasting, read the scriptures as a form of devotional reading. This will open your mind for hearing and receiving new insight, thoughts and ideas to meditate upon.

FOCUS

Focus your attention on God, not the issue or concern. Pray! Come before God with confidence that He will answer your prayer and meet your every need. Once you have given your concerns over to the Lord, release, let go and trust God. God can and God will do His part.

- *When Jehoshaphat received the report of, a great multitude coming against the nation of Judah,*

Jehoshaphat was afraid and turned his attention to seek the LORD, and proclaimed a fast throughout all Judah. So Judah gathered together to seek help from the Lord; they even came from all the cities of Judah to seek the Lord. (2 Chronicles 20:3-4 NASB)

- *Esther told Mordecai, "Go, gather together all the Jews who are in Susa, and fast for me. Do not eat or drink for three days, night or day. I and my attendants will fast as you do. When this is done, I will go to the king, even though it is against the law. And if I perish, I perish."* (Esther 4:16)

OUTCOMES

At the end of your fast expect God to give you an answer to your request.

- *Jesus said to the disciples... for assuredly, I say to you, if you have faith as a mustard seed, you will say to this mountain, 'Move from here to there, and it will move. Nothing will be impossible for you.* (Matthew 17:20)

A fast is declared in the book of Ezra as he was preparing to lead the people of Israel on their return to Jerusalem. Ezra sought the Lord for guidance, protection and peace. Before going to see the king, I was ashamed to ask the king for soldiers and horsemen to protect us from enemies on the road, because we had told the king,

"The gracious hand of our God is on everyone who looks to him, but his great anger is against all who forsake him." So we fasted and petitioned our God about this, and he answered our prayer. (Ezra 8:22-23)

DISCIPLINE AND COMMITMENT

But you be watchful in all things, endure afflictions, do the work of an evangelist, fulfill your ministry.
(2 Timothy 4:5 NKJV)

A successful fast requires two factors, discipline and commitment. Discipline and commitment means sacrificing time and energy to focus on things that are meaningful, fruitful and productive. After reading 2 Timothy 4: 1-8 what do you believe God wants you to work on? Choose to focus on one aspect and express your commitment in writing. This act alone will motivate the development of a disciplined spirit to strive harder with faith and determination. With God, you will succeed!

Commitment is paramount in every aspect of our spiritual, personal and relational life. An aspect of commitment includes having a disciplined prayer life. Your prayer life "must be fortified by a life aiming, unceasingly, to obey God, to attain conformity to the Divine Law, and to come into submission to the Divine will."[17] Throughout this time of prayer and fasting you are making a commitment to the Lord for spiritual guidance

---

[17] (Bounds 2006, 82)

on specific issues: (1) your life, (2) family, (3) church, (4) community, and (5) the world.

As you begin to confront every issue, there will be a transformation. The Lord will begin to rearrange your spiritual perspective on the issue(s) you have identified for your fast. During this process you are going to experience the magnificence of God in ways you have never imagined. The Lord will do His part by enhancing your spiritual life, if you remain disciplined and committed to the process.

Things to think about for a disciplined and committed life:

- List your desires, issues, problems and/or concerns.
- What sacrifices are you willing to make? What areas can you develop to enhance a discipline and committed life?
- List each independently.
- Write the date and time you propose to put your commitment into action.
- Pray over it and sign it.
- What discoveries did you realize while reading the selected scriptures? List as many as you can.
- What goals have you identified as a result of this process?

OWNING IT

***Work willingly at whatever you do, as
though you were working for the Lord rather
than for people.*** *(*Colossians 3:23 NLT)

Taking ownership over your fast, requires leaving those things behind you that are not beneficial to your spiritual life. You have to take personal responsibility over the promise you are making to the Lord. *He stores up sound wisdom for the upright; He is a shield to those who walk in integrity, Guarding the paths of justice, And He preserves the way of His godly ones.*[18]

We belong to God; we were purchased by the blood of Jesus. The very moment we accepted our salvation, we relinquished all rights to the things of the world and surrendered to the will of God.

MONITORING IT

***A man who makes a vow to the LORD
or makes a pledge... He must do exactly
what he said he would do.***
(Numbers 30:2 NLT)

In this scripture Moses summons the entire community of Israelites to make a vow to God. As you read and reflect on Numbers 30:2, examine your heart

---

[18] Proverbs 2:7-8 NASB

and answer the following questions. Write down your answers.

- What are the important elements in making a vow? List the important elements.
- How will you keep and monitor your commitment?
- Think about potential problems that might make it difficult to keep your commitment. What changes will you make to resolve these challenges?

As you write, let the Holy Spirit direct your thoughts.

MAINTAINING IT

Trust in the Lord with all your heart and lean not on your own understanding; in all your ways submit to Him, and He will make your paths straight.
(Proverbs 3:5-6)

No matter what the cost, your future and destiny are wrapped up in your commitment to God. You have to maintain the course. The road may not be easy; there will be times when temptation will meet you at your most vulnerable moments.

You will need to:

> *Put on the whole armor of God, that you may be able to stand against the wiles of the devil. For we do not wrestle against flesh and blood, but against principalities, against*

powers, against the rulers of the darkness of
this age, against spiritual hosts of wickedness
in the heavenly places. (Ephesians 6:11-12
NKJV)

Remember, the enemy desires to block and stop you from accomplishing what you stated you were going to do. However, come before the Lord with great expectation. Watch how the Lord will reshape and transform you spiritually and give you the desires of your heart. *So we fasted and petitioned our God about this, and he answered our prayer.* (Ezra 8:23)

While Ezra is a great example, there are many individuals throughout the Old Testament who fasted. Some were partial fasts and other individuals fasted for longer periods abstaining from food, and liquids. Moses, Samuel, Mordecai, David, Jehoshaphat, Isaiah, Elijah and many others held fasts. Even Jesus, when in the wilderness for forty days fasted. In every case we read in the Bible where the fast was spiritually motivated, the results of the fast provided godly wisdom and divine guidance. "More than any other spiritual discipline, fasting reveals the things that control us,"[19] whether it is people, places or things. "This is a wonderful benefit to the true disciple who longs to be transformed in to the image of Jesus Christ."[20] Daniel would not yield to temptation nor be seduced by the pleasures of the king's food and drink. Rather than jeopardize his relationship with God,

---

[19] (Foster 1988, 55)
[20] (Foster 1988, 55)

Daniel developed a healthier diet for himself and the three Hebrew boys. With the favor of God upon his life, Daniel was able to succeed in pleasing God and the king. Fasting was more than a physical exercise for them. It was a spiritual discipline and commitment to God.

Invest time in your fast and take charge over your life. Do not wait for anyone to motivate and encourage you. Never underestimate what you can do when you put your trust in God. As you are fasting and tearing down strongholds of adversity, depression, bad relationships, unhealthy eating, and spending habits, healing and transformation will begin to change your life. You will discover the power and the anointing of the Holy Spirit working within you. Your prayer life and time spent with the Lord will be enriched with a newness and freshness of peace that will surpass even your understanding.

JOURNALING IT

How do you journal? There is no right or wrong way of journaling. It is a powerful tool that allows for open dialogue with yourself while evaluating your life. Journaling helps you recognize positive behaviors; as well as negative behaviors that require change, modification or elimination. Remember you will never move from where you are spiritually until you are willing to acknowledge the areas that are hindering your spiritual growth. You should make every effort to journal each day. Set time aside to reflect and write freely. Also, at the end of the week summarize your new insights, experiences, progress and even setbacks. Consider the following journaling suggestions:

- Spiritual insights you have received during your fasting, prayer and personal meditation.
- Experiences that have inspired you.
- Happenings in your life and areas that you believe require assessment and potential change.
- Spiritual references and scriptures. Explain what they mean to you.
- Prayers of thanks, forgiveness and praise.
- Grateful lists - (Various lists can detail all the things you are grateful for.)

How should you begin your journaling? The following ideas will assist you in the journaling process:

- Try to eliminate distractions and begin your journaling experience by praying. Pray and acknowledge God's presence; remembering to ask the Holy Spirit to open your mind, heart and spirit during this writing experience.
- Date the entry and time. Begin by writing freely; as thoughts come to you write them down. Ask yourself questions. You might consider discussing your feelings, convictions, perplexing issues, experiences and attitudes.
- Set spiritual goals with a beginning and end date. These goals can be activities you desire to do on a daily, weekly or monthly basis.

- After writing your entry, review what you have written. End your journal entry with a prayer of gratitude. Thank God for insight and resolution. You might begin with this: Lord this time with you has been...

Finally, journaling has tremendous benefits. Journaling provides an emotional release while promoting mindfulness and increased self-awareness. But most importantly, this reflective activity will assist you in developing a deeper relationship with Jesus while making sense of your life.

Chapter 3

PREPARING FOR THE FAST

Brothers and sisters, I do not consider myself yet to have taken hold of it. But one thing I do: Forgetting what is behind and straining toward what is ahead, I press on toward the goal to win the prize for which God has called me heavenward in Christ Jesus. (Philippians 3:13-14)

PREPARING FOR THE FAST

Preparing for the fast is as important as the fast itself. Your body and mind must be prepared to take on this awesome spiritual journey. No two individuals are the same. Each person must take personal inventory of their body. Medical challenges, as well as physical challenges, will impact your approach and your desired outcome. Make sure you understand your limitations.

A successful fast must be carefully planned. Take time to plan a daily menu and do your research. When entering into a fast there are two critical factors. You must be physically able and spiritually willing for the challenge. If you are not sure of your physical limitations, seek medical advice and spiritual guidance. Begin praying for divine wisdom and understanding. This requires intimate sessions with God. Let the Lord know the desires of your heart. *The Lord will guide you always; he will satisfy your needs and strengthen your frame. You will be like a well-watered garden, like a spring whose waters never fail.* (Isaiah 58:11)

You will need to be mentally prepared if you want to win the battles of life. You will not win if you are not prepared. Your training requires due diligence and discipline. The Word must become food when you're hungry and water when you're thirsty.

Spiritual and mental preparation is viewing your problem from every direction. You need to know the depth, the length, and magnitude of what you are up against. Every battle is different, and every enemy is not the same. Some obstacles you must go around; some you have to go right through; and others you must attack from above. It's all about preparing yourself in advance. The Lord will show you what to do.

DIET

So the guard took away their choice food and
the wine they were to drink and gave
them vegetables instead.
(Daniel 1:16)

Never under estimate the power of faith and fasting. Daniel's faith in God gave him confidence that eating the right foods would make him and the three Hebrew boys healthier. He challenged the servant after ten days to compare the Hebrews to the individuals who ate the king's delicacies. Daniel's was so convincing that the king's servant consented and gave them permission to fast and eat as requested. At the completion of the fast, Daniel and the three Hebrew boys were far healthier in body and mind than all the young men who ate from the king's table.

Having healthy bodies are a part of God's divine plan. We over indulge, habitually eating foods that are unhealthy. As a result we are plagued with every sickness and disease. Instead of good health, we suffer with various physical complications and face early death. *Do you not know that your bodies are temples of the Holy Spirit, who is in you, whom you have received from God?*

You are not your own; (1 Corinthians 6:19). Having a healthy diet is fundamental in fasting and living well. Our unique bodies have the ability to heal itself when we eat proper foods, exercise and receive the necessary sleep needed for our bodies.

Fasting is a great way to eliminate, cleanse, and purify the body from toxic waste. If you are serious about getting the most out of your fast, learn as much as you can from books, health magazines and professional individuals. Health food stores have excellent resources and individuals who are well trained in healthy living, eating, and dieting. Eating the right foods will protect and combat your body from disease, stress, fatigue, mood swings and control your weight. It will also stimulate your mind and improve brain functioning. Prior to your fast, at least three days in advance, begin reducing the amount of food you eat. You should focus on adding foods to your diet, such as: nuts, fresh fruits, fresh vegetables, and natural juices to prepare your body. Remember to drink plenty of water and stay away from processed foods and sugar. If you have medical challenges, consult your physician.

There are many recommendations for planning a healthy menu for your fast. Once you decide upon fasting begin to:

1. Organize and plan your meals for the entire week breakfast, lunch and dinner.
2. Include your family when organizing and planning the menu.

3. Prepare a list of each of the major food groups (i.e. fruits, vegetables, grains, protein and dairy).

4. Eliminate foods you want to avoid. This will become the core foundation for meal planning and preparation.

5. Create menus with food themes to bring excitement to your fast. You can be creative with a variation of soups, salads, whole grains and beans for different days of the week.

6. Designate specific times for each meal of the day.

7. Enjoy healthy snacks that will not alter your diet. Sliced fruit and vegetables (i.e. carrots, celery, zucchini, broccoli, tomatoes and edamames) are all great healthy snacks.

8. Journal your entire experience. It is important to reflect on the physical, mental and spiritual effects from the foods you eat. If the results are promising, it may suggest to you a new way of eating for healthy living.

9. Save your menu, share it with others!

SCRIPTURE PREPARATION

***All Scripture is breathed out by God and
profitable for teaching, for reproof, for
correction, and for training in righteousness.***
(2 Timothy 3:16 ESV)

Choosing the right scriptures and a daily mediation plan is extremely important. You will never know what God desires for your life if you are not willing to take time to read and study His Word. God's Word is the most important aspect of maintaining a well-balanced life and having a successful fast. It is filled with examples, solutions, prayers, warnings, counsel, wisdom and so much more to help guide and direct you through every stage of your journey. *Like new born babies, you must crave spiritual milk so that you will grow into a full experience of salvation.*

Cry out for this nourishment,[21] and the inspired Word of God will minister to your every need as it has done for so many in ages past. Take time to research which scriptures you will read in the morning and evening. Be mindful to *"Keep this Book of the Law always on your lips; meditate on it day and night, so that you may be careful to do everything written in it. Then you will be prosperous and successful."*[22]

If you are unsure of what to read for your particular fast, there are many books and websites available to assist you through this process. Included in this book and assigned lessons are daily and weekly meditations with suggested scriptures to read.

Remember you are seeking spiritual guidance, healing, deliverance, and a closer walk with God. A well designed plan for reading and studying the Word will help you maintain a spiritual focus.

SELECTING THE RIGHT TIME FOR PRAYER AND FASTING

In the early morning, while it was still dark, Jesus got up, left the house, and went away to a secluded place, and was praying there. (Mark 1:35 NASB)

A spiritual fast should have a start and finish. There should be time designated for prayer, reading, meditating, walking, eating, and sleeping. The more disciplined and

---

[21] 1 Peter 2:2 NLT
[22] Joshua 1:8 NIV

committed you are, the more effective your fast will be. Do not allow your time for prayer and fasting to be compromised or minimized. God is not looking for super heroes, but those who are faithful.

The Bible does not prescribe the time or length of prayer, but it does offer guidelines. "In Psalm 88, prayer is offered in the early morning (v. 13), and Psalm 55, prayers are said morning, noon, and evening (v. 17). The author of Psalm 119 advocates prayer seven times a day (v. 164). Daniel knelt for devotions three times a day (Daniel 6:10). Jesus prayed before sunrise (Mark 1:35) and in the evening when the day's work was over (Mark 6:46). Peter prayed at the third, sixth, and ninth hours."[23] For a Christian, prayer should be a natural way of life, not just for times of crisis, moments of need or simply to guide you through a fast.

WORKING THROUGH PROBLEMS

Dear brothers and sisters, when troubles of any kind come your way, consider it an opportunity for great joy. For you know that when your faith is tested, your endurance has a chance to grow. So let it grow, for when your endurance is fully developed, you will be perfect and complete, needing nothing. (James 1:2-4 NLT)

---

[23] Bolesch 1988

In life, there are both successes and failures. At times we are able to accomplish what we set out to do; and at other times, for whatever reason, we find ourselves not being able to achieve our goals. Sometimes our ambitions are too high and at other times there are uncontrollable circumstances that prevent us from succeeding.

During your fast you may be faced with some difficult situations that may prevent you from completing your goal and objective. Do not become discouraged. You are not the first and certainly will not be the last who will begin this spiritual journey and not complete it on time. However, you must remain focused. When your motives are pure and your intentions are right you will discover that there is nothing you will not be able to accomplish through the counsel of God.

As soon as you can define the problem, there is an even greater opportunity for you to find a solution. Get back on track. Individuals want to be free of problems. However, the problem you long to be free of may actually be designed to shape and develop you. Ultimately helping you become what the Lord has destined for your life. At the same time keep in mind not every problem will be solved through fasting and prayer. In the process you will gain wisdom, deeper spiritual insight and understanding about who you are and the God of our Salvation.

Chapter 4

RENEWAL, DEDICATION
AND COMMITMENT

Search me, O God, and know my heart; test
my thoughts. Point out anything you find in
me that makes you sad, and lead me along
the path of everlasting life.
(Psalm 139:23-24 TLB)

RENEWAL, DEDICATION AND COMMITMENT

O God, You are my God; Early will I seek you; My soul thirsts for You; My flesh longs for You in a dry and thirsty land where there is no water. (Psalm 63:1 NKJV)

Prayer:

I am focusing all my attention on my relationship with my Lord and Savior Jesus Christ. Each morning and evening while meditating on Your Word, I will make it a priority to take personal inventory of my life. In my quest for wholeness, healing and transformation I will seek Your Word for ways I can draw closer to you.

During this special time for your spiritual renewal, rededication and commitment, you should stop and take a personal inventory. Ask yourself are you content with where you are and what God desires for your life. As a Christian, the very foundation of what we believe is connected to our faith in God. We should never settle for less than what we were created to be. If we are going to soar like an eagle, expand our territory and reach higher heights, we cannot afford to be overwhelmed and influenced with the negatives of life. Allow the Holy Spirit to inspire, empower and guide you. I encourage each of you to seek the Lord, even in small things. Nothing is insignificant for the Lord. There is more in store for your life than you can ever imagine. The trials and challenges you face are common themes that will eventually play out over time. They will mold and shape your destiny. The very things - faith, trust and confidence that kept others in ages past, will be the same things that will keep you.

Stay connected to Jesus during your fast. To do so you must practice and persevere through prayer. Jesus never grew tired of inviting, promoting, encouraging and commanding us to pray. Prayer was the spiritual air that Jesus breathed every day of His life. He practiced an unending communion between Himself and the Father. He urged His disciples to do the same. He said, *Be always on the watch, and pray that you may be able to escape all that is about to happen, and that you may be able to stand before the Son of Man."* (Luke 21:36) Our teacher in life and ministry, Jesus is the example you must follow to remain connected to the source of God's love and power during your spiritual journey.

NEVER GIVE UP

God is looking for the opportunity to bless your life. Do not be anxious about anything. Remember, this is a spiritual journey, not a race. Anxious thoughts and desires often times take you out of the will of God, causing you to fall short of your desired goal.

You must practice being patient. When you are patient you will receive blessings beyond your understanding. It is a win- win situation for both the petitioner and the supplier. In this case, our supplier is Jesus Christ. He has access to all you need to complete your spiritual journey and fast. Be encouraged and never give up hope. Keep working and striving to be the best. God is not through with developing your life no matter how difficult things are. Charles Spurgeon reminds us, "Christ is the builder of His spiritual temple, and He is building it on the mountains of His unchangeable love, His omnipotent grace and His infallible truth."[24]

Pray unceasingly, stand up and be counted. It is through prayer that you hear God's voice and see the mighty works of His hands. Prayer will draw you closer to God's heart who will pour into your soul, perfect peace. Pray with expectation and see what God will do through you. At the end of every storm, trial and difficulty there is a brighter day. After every battle there is victory. **YOU CAN MAKE IT!**

---

[24] (Reimann 2008, 174)

FASTING GOALS AND OBJECTIVES:

Before you begin to fast:

- List and identify personal challenges you desire to overcome.
- List spiritual goals.

Personal Challenges	Spiritual Goals

Spiritual Focus:

During your morning and evening prayer and meditation utilize this time wisely to focus on your personal challenges and spiritual goals. The Lord desires to hear from you. I sought the *LORD, and he answered me; he delivered me from all my fears.* (Psalm 34:4)

Morning Readings

Sunday	Ephesians	2:1-10
Monday	Romans	2:1-21
Tuesday	Philippians	4:4-8
Wednesday	1 Peter	5:6-11
Thursday	Psalm	51:1-11
Friday	Psalm	139:1-3, 23-24

Evening Readings

Sunday	Isaiah	43:1-7
Monday	Psalm	27:4-10
Tuesday	1 Timothy	6:6-16
Wednesday	1 Corinthians	2:12-16
Thursday	Psalm	37:23-29
Friday	Psalm	40:1-5

SATURDAY MORNING
A PRAYER WALK WITH GOD
Genesis 41:1-44

Meditation Focus:

Sometimes God places us in surroundings and situations we do not understand. Other times we may lose all we have, in order to become who God created us to be. Joseph was sold into slavery by his brothers. He was lied on and accused for a crime he did not commit. In the midst of this remarkable journey of trials and tribulations God opened an amazing door of opportunity for Joseph to realize his greatest potential.

We all have a history and a future. There is always a yesterday and tomorrow, a beginning and end. Likewise there is a difference between a caterpillar and a butterfly. There are stages a caterpillar goes through before it is transformed into the beautiful butterfly. The same is true for each of us. We go through stages of life that are sometimes totally uncomfortable and even undesirable. However, at the right moment in time you will begin to transform from a baby, to a young child, to a teen and then an adult. Within each stage of your life, if you are in the right spiritual place an even greater transformation will take place.

Whatever dreams and ambitions you have, God will give you both strength and power to accomplish them. Nothing will be able to block you. Your past, present, and future are all interconnected to who you are and what God has purposed for your life!

The focus of your prayer walk is for individual spiritual renewal, dedication, and commitment to God. As you are praying and walking, ask the Lord to tear down every wall of opposition in your life: discontent, sadness, anger, frustration, poor self-esteem, depression, and idleness. Be honest with yourself!

When you have been chosen and given a part in God's divine plan, your qualifications or lack of, have little to do with the circumstances in and around your life. Physical conditions cannot control the spirit of a person who chooses not to be imprisoned. Spiritual discipline devoted to prayer and meditation will release shackles of oppression, depression, lift heavy burdens of despair, and give hope in your darkest hours of life.

Lift up your heads, O you gates! And be lifted up, you everlasting doors! And the King of glory shall come in. Who is this King of Glory? The Lord strong and mighty, the Lord mighty in battle. (Psalm 24:7-8 NKJV)

Prayer:
Lord, I pray you will continue to renew and refresh my mind with your spirit of truth, beauty and love. Anoint me with creativity, new ideas, thoughts, vision and energy to be the best in all I do. When I am weak and weary, when my mind, body and spirit is troubled and tired, help me to find rest and comfort in you. I speak your peace, grace and perfect order into every encounter and conversation. Amen.

Spiritual Outcome:

Now that you have identified the purpose of your fast, and your spiritual focus, be specific on your desired outcomes and new insights you are expecting to learn and/or receive. What changes are you hoping for?

Desired Outcomes - New Insights Changes

Summarize What You Have Learned This Week

How Did Meditation, Fasting and Prayer Impact Your Life This Week?

Follow Through:

One of the most important aspect of a fast is the follow through. After the Lord has given you new insight and revelation to your problems or concerns there must be a willingness and a commitment to act and complete the fasting process.

- Think through your strategy.
- How will you implement what you have learned during this week?

Implementation Plan

Chapter 5

PUTTING GOD FIRST THE FAMILY'S WEEK OF PRAYER AND FASTING

The family has fulfilled God's intent to provide context for creation and care in order to ensure the continuity of humankind.
(H. Anderson)

Putting God First The Family's Week of Prayerand Fasting

Teach them to your children, talking about them when you sit at home and when you walk along the road, when you lie down and when you get up.
(Deuteronomy 11:19)

Prayer:

This week I am praying and fasting for my family. Lord build and strengthen our spiritual lives individually and collectively. It is my prayer that strongholds of division, jealousy and strive will be destroyed. Open our hearts to receive healing, restoration, deliverance, love, peace and salvation. I say, "Believe in the Lord Jesus Christ, and you will be saved, you and your household." (Acts 16:31)

Our families are a great blessing and an asset to our lives.

For better or worst, they make and shape who we are by laying the foundation for our present and future. In this divinely arranged union by God, we find and develop a multitude of feelings and experiences: love, joy, happiness, heartaches, and disappointments. While none of us have a perfect family, there are unique memories, experiences, moments, and encounters that we share with those whom God has blessed to be an intricate part of our lives.

The dynamics in our families are always changing as the family grows. Some are expected and others are not. The process of adaptability and acceptability affects each individual family member differently, while impacting the entire family. We are excited watching our children grow and develop as they transition through the various stages of their lives. We try to accept and adapt to the peaks and valleys in our relationship with our spouses. But what is difficult to adapt and accept are not the transitioning or the peaks and valleys. It is the personalities and characteristics that comes with the transformation of the old person we once knew, to the new individual we do not understand.

There are no single answers, however, there are positive biblical solutions (i.e. love, compassion, kindness, and forgiveness) that will help heal and strengthen the family unit and improve relationships. For too long we allowed the enemy to have control of what God has blessed and ordained as good. Every member of the family can maintain their own independent identity while seeking to put God first. *If a house is divided against itself, that house cannot stand.* (Mark 3:25). Pray, focus and fast for family unity, bonding in every relationship, spiritual protection and divine guidance for all. A family that prays together will stay together!

Fasting Goals and Objectives:

Before you begin to fast:

- List and identify individual concerns for the family.
- List and identify your desired outcomes for your the family.

Objectives for Individual Family Members	Objectives for the Entire Family

Spiritual Focus:

During your morning and evening prayer and meditation, utilize this time wisely to focus on each prayer objective for individual family members and the entire family. This is not a time to hold back, make your prayers and petitions known to God.

Morning Readings

Sunday	Joshua	24:14-15
Monday	Psalm	78:1-8
Tuesday	Exodus	20:1-17
Wednesday	Deuteronomy	6:4-8
Thursday	Genesis	18:19
Friday	Joshua	2:12-14; 6:22-25

Evening Readings

Sunday	Ephesians	5:15-33; 6:1-4
Monday	Titus	2:1-6
Tuesday	Matthew	18:19-20
Wednesday	Acts	16:30-33
Thursday	1 Timothy	3:4; 5:8
Friday	1 Samuel	2:27-28

Saturday Morning A Prayer Walk with God

(Ephesians 5:22-33; 6:1-3)

Meditation Focus:

You cannot hold what you believe loosely; your faith must be taken seriously. When the head of the house begins to take control of their house by teaching the principles of godliness and righteousness with the same kind of love Christ has for the church, the entire family will be blessed.

No matter how challenging the problems or how difficult the situation may be, make every effort to hold onto your faith.

Your faith must become your whole armor of God that protects you and your family *against principalities, against powers, against the rulers of darkness in this world, and against spiritual wickedness in high places.* (Ephesians 6:12)

Our prayer walk focus for this week is dealing with walls of opposition in your family - strife, tension, disobedience, disrespect and divorce. The focus of this prayer walk is for spiritual breakthroughs, unity, and peace within your family. Discuss the concerns placed on your heart with family members. Your prayer walk should begin in your house. Walk through every room in your house, praying and asking God to release every shackle and stronghold.

Prayer:

Lord, I acknowledge Your Lordship over all that will be spoken, thought, decided, and accomplished in my life; in the life of my children, loved ones and family. I am grateful for the blessings of these precious gifts. These gifts of affection demonstrate your love for me. I do not take them lightly. I commit them to you.

Spiritual Outcome:

Now that you have identified the purpose of your fast, and your spiritual focus, be specific on your desired outcomes and new insights you are expecting to learn and/or receive. What changes are you hoping for?

Desired Outcomes - New Insights Changes

Summarize What You Have Learned This Week

How Did Meditation, Fasting and Prayer Impact Your Life This Week?

Follow Through:

One of the most important aspect of a fast is the follow through. After the Lord has given you new insight and revelation to your problems or concerns there must be a willingness and a commitment to act and complete the fasting process.

- Think through your strategy.
- How will you implement what you have learned during this week?

Implementation Plan

Chapter 6

BUILDING THE BODY OF CHRIST

**The real spiritual life must be horizontal as
well as vertical; spread more and more
as well as aspire more and more.**
(Evelyn Underhill)

BUILDING THE BODY OF CHRIST

As a member you are no longer strangers and foreigners, but fellow citizens with the saints and members of the household of God. (Ephesians 2:19)

Prayer:

Lord my assignment this week is to meditate on your Word, for spiritual insight and divine guidance. Please empower and encourage the leadership and membership of the body of Christ to be an inclusive, effective and an active spiritual body. While praying, fasting, and working together with other believers, Lord speak to my life. Allow me to make a difference in the life of my church. Amen.

Currently, there is no common ground in our communities and the world. The forces that divide us also threatens to destroy us. We are divided by conflicting political beliefs, racial tension, economic disparity, cultural differences and social injustice not only in the world, but also within the body of Christ.

When we look at the declining numbers of individuals attending church, it is evident that we have become wiser in the things of the world and weaker in the things of God. In this twenty-first century of modern technology we have learned to communicate with one another through every form of social media. We can send men and women to the moon; a spaceship to Mars; and launch satellites to orbit the earth. Nevertheless we see devastations, tragedies, relentless atrocities, violence and evil acts of aggression in our world. It is unmistakably obvious to those who are in Christ that our condition is so perilous one cannot help but ask the question, *Can these bones live?* (Ezekiel 37:3)

When describing the exalted position of Jesus, the Apostle Paul explained that the church is the "Body of Christ" and Jesus is the head of this body. *We are His workmanship, created in Christ Jesus for good works, which God prepared beforehand that we should walk in them.* (Ephesians 2:10) It is the ultimate expectation of God that Christians live out their faith in such a way that non-believers would be drawn to Christ.

What does the Lord require of you? (Micah 6:8) As the church seeks to live out its faith by doing the will of the Lord, it must demonstrate a willing spirit to open its doors and allow the power of the Holy Spirit to abide where people can: (1) worship a God that is completely above human limitations; (2) find hope, salvation and reconcile their broken relationships with God and one another; and (3) demonstrate the manifestation of God's character and ultimate power, transcendence, and moral perfection to the world. In answer to the question presented to Ezekiel, yes, these dry bones can live when God is in the midst of building the body of Christ.

Fasting Goals and Objectives:

Before you begin to fast:

- List and identify individual concerns for the leadership and membership of your local church.
- List and identify your desired outcomes.

Individual Concerns	Desired Outcomes

Spiritual Focus:

Utilize this time wisely to focus on your concerns and desired outcomes for the leadership and membership of the church.

This is not a time to hold back. *Make your prayers and your petitions known to God.* (Philippians 4:6). *For everyone who asks receives; he who seeks finds; and to him who knocks, the door will be opened.* (Matthew 7:8)

Morning Readings

Sunday	1 Corinthians	12:4-29
Monday	Ephesians	4:11-32
Tuesday	Acts	2:36-47
Wednesday	Philippians	4:14-20
Thursday	2 Peter	1:1-11
Friday	John	20:19-23

Evening Readings

Sunday	Exodus	35:1-29
Monday	2 Chronicles	7:1-11
Tuesday	Isaiah	6:1-8
Wednesday	Nehemiah	4:1-14
Thursday	Haggai	1:2-14
Friday	Malachi	3:1-12

Saturday Morning A Prayer Walk with God

Nehemiah 4:1-23

Meditation Focus:

Nehemiah saw the need to rebuild the wall that had been broken and the gates that were burned. Under much opposition, he rallied the people together on a common cause and completed the work.

On this prayer walk, you are encouraged to join with others to pray for specific goals on how the church can work together to accomplish its mission and purpose. Focus your thoughts on unity in the body and on... "those things that are true, honest, just, pure, lovely, of good report, virtuous and praiseworthy." (See Philippians 4:8) Ask the Lord to give the church every resource required to meet the needs of the people. You must stir up your faith and the faith of other members within the body of Christ.

The work Christ has given to the church is never ending. It is a ministry that requires commitment, faithfulness, endurance and perseverance. God chose you! He expects you to be faithful and committed to working in unity with other believers towards kingdom building. Pray, meditate, ask and seek God's guidance for you and your local church.

Prayer:

Lord, "the harvest is plentiful but the laborers are few." (Matthew 9:37) Empower our church with a compassionate willing spirit for mission, ministry, and the work of building the body of Christ!

Spiritual Outcomes:

Now that you have identified the purpose of your fast, and your spiritual focus, be specific on your desired outcomes and new insights you are expecting to learn and/or receive. What changes are you hoping for?

Desired Outcomes - New Insights Changes

Summarize What You Have Learned This Week

How Did Meditation, Fasting and Prayer Impact Your Life This Week?

Follow Through:

One of the most important aspect of a fast is the follow through. After the Lord has given you new insight and revelation to your problems or concerns, there must be a willingness and a commitment without reservation to act upon and complete the fasting process.

- Think through your strategy.
- How will you implement what you have learned during this week?

Implementation Plan

Chapter 7

BRIDGING THE
GAP BETWEEN

CHURCH AND COMMUNITY

BRIDGING THE GAP BETWEEN CHURCH AND COMMUNITY

Prayer:

Hear my prayer O God! As we call on Your name, we are approaching your throne of grace in expectation. We come to You for wisdom and in faith, for those who are in the church and community. We need your guidance, loving Father. Help our church serve our community! Where there are places of weakness, show us how to stand with our people to provide strength. Where there is pain, strengthen us to be a place of refuge. Where there is division, teach us to be peacemakers. Where there is confusion, help us bring clarity. With You, we know we can build our community to become a place where peace abides and where there is justice and equality for all people. Amen.

The church has always played a major role in our communities. It has traditionally been a sacred place and space where hopes and dreams are inspired and sustained.

Education is not enough to create the changes we need in our communities. There must be a solution to every need and every problem, as stated by Ann L. Nickson, "You must take the need and infirmities of others to heart as if they were your own, and offer your means as if they were theirs, just as Christ does for you."[25] The church is that place where God speaks clearly to the people from the pulpit to the pew, to the street, and into the lives of those who are

---

[25] (Nickson 2002,89)

seeking to find their way. As people today are trying to pass through this wilderness of exploitation, many who were once freed from bondage and addictions are once again finding themselves being enslaved.

Collectively, many of us are highly qualified in our respective academic and professional careers. We have more degrees than our parents. But without spiritual wisdom and divine intervention, unrealized potentialities will continue to remain undeveloped in individuals and our community. In order to bring about deliverance, healing, and restoration to people who are enslaved as a result of systemic injustices and generational institutionalized programs, a transformation must take place. If the church is serious about being all God called it to be, it cannot depend or wait for the world to change. The church is the only institution commissioned by God to bring hope, love and support to individuals within our communities who have been marginalized.

The church has been called to be a change agent for the Lord. Collectively in our decisions and actions we must seek the Lord. It is when we find Him in our lives, places of employment, schools, churches and families that we will bridge the gap between the church and community. During your time of fasting and praying, seek the Lord for divine council and guidance on how you can become a change agent for God! Your church and community needs you.

Fasting Goals and Objectives:

Before you begin to fast:

- List and identify community concerns.
- List and identify your desired outcomes for the church and community.

Community Concerns	Desired Goals for Church and Community

Spiritual Focus:

During your morning and evening prayer and meditation focus on the role of the church in bridging the gap between its community. The Lord desires to hear from you. *I sought the LORD, and he answered me; he delivered me from all my fears.* (Psalm 34:4)

Morning Readings

Sunday	Acts	2:36-46
Monday	Ephesians	4:11-32
Tuesday	John	4:1-30
Wednesday	John	4:31-42
Thursday	Psalm	73:23-28
Friday	Luke	10:30-37

Evening Readings

Sunday	Nehemiah	1:1-11
Monday	2 Chronicles	7:12-18
Tuesday	Ezekiel	37:1-14
Wednesday	Jonah	3:1-10
Thursday	Isaiah	42:1-8
Friday	Isaiah	43:1-13

Saturday Morning A Prayer Walk with God

(Nehemiah 2:12-13)

Meditation Focus:

Take time to ask God how you can assist the church in making a difference in your community. Position is the key to winning any battle. You must be in a place of stability and not insecurity. Take into account every opposition that has an adverse affect upon your church and community. This will become your fasting focus. Keep in mind, that you will not overcome these challenges if you are not in a spiritual position. The world is moving at an extremely fast pace; time is not your best friend. You do not have the physical endurance or the mental capacity to deal with all that is going on. Godly wisdom and spiritual discernment must be included in your life to deal with every opposition in your community. Then *no weapon formed against you shall prosper. And every tongue which rises against you in judgment You shall condemn. This is the heritage of the servants of the Lord, And their righteousness is from Me, Says the Lord.* (Isaiah 54:17 NKJV)

Pray for your community leaders, schools and businesses. Seek the Lord for guidance on how they can provide the necessary resources, wisdom, knowledge, skills, and ability to assist your church. Pray and fight for your brothers and sisters who are marginalized and underserved, for they are a part of the family of God.

Spiritual Outcomes:

Now that you have identified the purpose of your fast,and your spiritual focus, be specific on your desired outcomes and new insights you are expecting to learn and/or receive. What changes are you hoping for?

Desired Outcomes - New Insights Changes

Summarize What You Have Learned This Week

How Did Meditation, Fasting and Prayer Impact Your Life This Week?

Follow Through:

One of the most important aspect of a fast is the follow through. After the Lord has given you new insight and revelation to your problems or concerns there must be a willingness and a commitment without reservation to act upon and complete the fasting process.

- Think through your strategy.
- How will you implement what you have learned during this week?

Implementation Plan

Chapter 8

WORLD TRANSFORMATION

Whenever we are faced with any calamity such as war, disease or famine, we can come to stand in Your presence before this Temple where Your name is honored. We can cry out to You to save us, and You will hear us and rescue us.
(2 Chronicles 20:9 NLT)

WORLD TRANSFORMATION

Prayer:

I thank you God for the joy of my salvation. I recognize as a Christian that I am blessed. I understand my blessings are not to be used selfishly but to be shared with others. It is my prayer that you will empower me with compassion and love. Guide my heart, mind and spirit to do what is right in our world. Help me bring about peaceful solutions and world transformation. Amen.

There is no greater time than the present for every Christian to seek the Lord and remain faithful to the promise, *If my people who are called by My name will humble themselves, and pray and seek My face, and turn from their wicked ways, then I will hear from heaven, and will forgive their sin and heal their land.* (2 Chronicles 7:14) There are a plethora of issues: (world hunger, poverty, disease, active wars, rumors of wars, immigration, global warming, air, land and water pollution, racism, social injustice, drugs, gangs, violence and crime) that plague the world. The church has a moral and spiritual responsibility to confront and address each of these issues.

Each of us have the power through God to make a difference. We are our brother's and sister's keeper. The hurt, pain, and devastations we are seeing and experiencing in our world today are the results of moral and spiritual abandonment. All life in this world is interconnected, whether it is the bird that sings, the grass that grows, or the fish that swims in the rivers and seas. Everything in the heavens, everything that roams and grows on the earth, everything in all of God's creation was made to give glory to God.

You must pray for the world. Prayer changes things. As you fast and pray, pray for world leaders and governments. Ask God to provide them with compassion instead of a need to control; peace instead of power; and love in place of war. As you seek God, ask the Lord to change leaders' hearts, seek solutions, and resources to help eradicate the disparities of hunger, poverty, social injustice, immigration and environmental issues that plague our world. Whatever you are praying for let God use you. *Pray without ceasing.* (1Thessalonians 5:17) *Offer to God a sacrifice of thanksgiving, and perform your vows to the Most High, and call upon Me in the day of trouble; I will deliver you, and you shall glorify Me.* (Psalm 50:14-15)

Fasting Goals and Objectives:

Before you begin to fast:
- List and identify your concerns for the world.
- List and identify your desired outcomes for world transformation.

World Concerns	Desired Goals for World Transformation

Spiritual Focus:

During your morning and evening prayer and meditation utilize this time wisely to focus on world transformation challenges and spiritual goals. *There is neither Jew nor Gentile, neither slave nor free, nor is there male and female, for you are all one in Christ Jesus.* (Galatians 3:28)

Morning Readings

Sunday	Psalm	46:1-11
Monday	Psalm	49:1-8
Tuesday	John	3:16-24
Wednesday	Mark	16:15-20
Thursday	Acts	2:1-11
Friday	Isaiah	11:1-11

Evening Readings

Sunday	Romans	15:1-10
Monday	Luke	14.15-24
Tuesday	1 Peter	3:8-20
Wednesday	Matthew	28:16-20
Thursday	Psalm	24:1-2
Friday	Revelation	7:1-17

Saturday Morning A Prayer Walk With God.

Isaiah 1:16-20

Meditation Focus:

This prayer walk focuses on world transformation. In the presence of the Lord we are one. Only the arrogant and the proud boast in themselves, but the humble are exalted by God. Let us work together as one towards world transformation.

The Psalmist ask this question, after all the many blessing he had received from the Lord, *What shall I render unto the Lord for all his benefits toward me?* (Psalm 116:12 KJV) One way to make a difference in the life of others is by helping bring about world transformation. It is not about what you have, but what you do with what God has given you. Moses had this dilemma when he stood before the Red Sea with the children of Israel and nowhere to go. Pharaoh and his army were in strong pursuit of trying to stop Moses and the Israelites from leaving Egypt. Going back was not an option. Moses' only option was to move forward. However, it was not until God reminded Moses of what was in his hand. With this simple reminder, the task which seemed impossible became doable. It gave Moses the ability to move the people forward towards the promise land. Moses stretched out his rod and parted the waters. It opened a passage for the people to cross to the other side. (See Exodus 14). World transformation begins with each of us using what God has given us to make a difference in the life of others.

> *Prayer:*
>
> *Dear God, may all I do with my family, church, and community to engage and educate those around me be used in concert with the many voices in our world. Hear our prayer for peace, the end of injustice, discrimination against immigrants, religious beliefs, people of color, human trafficking, and political oppression. Let our resounding voices change our world for the better! Amen.*

Spiritual Outcome:

Now that you have identified the purpose of your fast, and your spiritual focus, be specific on your desired outcomes and new insights you are expecting to learn and/or receive. What changes are you hoping for?

Desired Outcomes - New Insights Changes

Summarize What You Have Learned This Week

How Did Meditation, Fasting and Prayer Impact Your Life This Week?

Follow Through:

One of the most important aspect of a fast is the follow through. After the Lord has given you new insight and revelation to your problems or concerns there must be a willingness and a commitment without reservation to act upon and complete the fasting process.

- Think through your strategy.
- How will you implement what you have learned during this week?

Implementation Plan

Chapter 9

HEALING AND RESTORATION

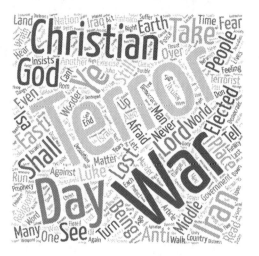

It is not surprising to find out that there are innumerable Christians who are more eager to discuss their pain and healing than their sin and salvation.
(Andrew Sung Park)

HEALING AND RESTORATION

Prayer:

Gracious God, Creator and Sustainer of life, the pain I feel from the despair and the overwhelming atrocities that plague our world is real... not only in my life but in the lives of so many. As I lift my voice in prayer, I seek wisdom, knowledge and understanding from You. Your power and love is incomprehensible. O God you fashioned the world with your hands, and spoke into existence the creative order of the universe. May You once again allow the dew drops of heavenly grace and mercy shower me with spiritual vigor! Equip me with a willing desire to work with others to bring healing and restoration to our world! Amen.

The world is on the verge of a trauma pandemic. The contrary winds of discrimination, turbulent waves of injustice, and merciless acts of oppression has placed fear into the hearts of the people in our nation and world. Our streets and communities are filled with blood, divisiveness, hatred, bigotry, anger, uncertainty, dismay, drug addiction, immorality, and discontent. Individuals are afraid and hurt from mental, emotional and physical abuse. We have become too comfortable, as if it is the norm to witness individuals' rights being eroded and violated. Gender discrimination, elder abuse, child abuse, racism, classicism, gang violence, police brutality and killings are prevalent. These stories of violations and pain fill the televised news hours, pages of the newspapers and internet.

Our society is technologically advanced. Yet, the world with all of its modern technology has not found solutions for those who are hurting and in need of healing. For some, operations, medical procedures, over-the-counter medications, prescription drugs and various therapies help eliminate and control the pain. However, these remedies do not offer healing to a wounded spirit, a bruised soul or respond to the desolation of spiritual despair. This dilemma is not new. Jesus told his perplexed disciples, who failed to deliver a person from possession of an evil spirit, *This kind can come out by nothing but prayer and fasting.*[26] Jesus in this simple sentence reminded his disciples of several key points which we must consider. The disciples witnessed Jesus delivering individuals with persistent demonic spirits. They assumed that they could cast out the demon just like Jesus, but they were wrong. Their challenge came with their failure to recognize as simply stated by Jesus, *Some things come through fasting and prayer.*

As Christians, we must communicate with God. Aligning with the power of the Holy Spirit is to reconnect and seek the face and heart of God. When we communicate and listen to God, the Holy Spirit gives us power to move mountains.

Let us fast and pray together for healing and restoration in our communities, nation and world. Pray in the privacy of your home. Pray on your way to work; as you enter the sanctuary and with other believers. Ask God! Wait on God! Respond to God!

---

[26] (Mark 9:28-29)

Fasting Goals and Objectives:

Before you begin to fast:

* List healing and restoration concerns.
* List desired outcomes: individual, family, church, community and world.

Healing and Restoration Concerns	Desired Goals for Restoration

Spiritual Focus:

During your morning and evening prayer and meditation utilize this time wisely to focus on your personal challenges and spiritual goals. The Lord desires to hear from you.

Morning Readings

Sunday	Acts	2:36-46
Monday	Ephesians	4:11-32
Tuesday	John	4:1-30
Wednesday	John	4:31-42
Thursday	Luke	4:4-19
Friday	Luke	10:30-37

Evening Readings

Sunday	Nehemiah	1:1-11
Monday	2 Chronicles	7:12-18
Tuesday	Ezekiel	37:1-14
Wednesday	John	3:1-10
Thursday	Isaiah	42:1-8
Friday	Isaiah	43:1-13

Saturday Morning A Prayer Walk With God

(Isaiah 61:1)

And Jesus went about all Galilee, teaching in their synagogues, preaching the gospel of the kingdom and healing all kinds of sickness and all kinds of diseases among the people. Then His fame went throughout all Syria; and they brought to Him all sick people who were afflicted with various diseases and torments, and those who were demon possessed, epileptics, and paralytics; and He healed them. Great multitudes followed Him – from Galilee, and from Decapolis, Jerusalem, Judea, and beyond the Jordan. (Matthew 4:23-25)

Meditation Focus:

This prayer walk will focus on healing. Ask God to help you fulfill your personal calling in this world. Seek God's guidance on how you can work together with those in your church, community, and around the world to heal and transform broken lives.

Spiritual Outcome:

Now that you have identified the purpose of your fast, and your spiritual focus, be specific on your desired outcomes and the new insights you are expecting to learn and/or receive. What changes are you hoping for?

Prayer:

Lord, our world is overwhelmed with never ending moments of violence, wars, abuse, and hatred. We seek your divine intervention and stand together in agreement with the promises as written in Your Word, "If my people, who are called by my name, will humble themselves and pray and seek my face and turn from their wicked ways, then I will hear from heaven, and I will forgive their sin and will heal their land." Hear our prayer, O Lord, for bringing about healing and restoration in our world. Amen.

Desired Outcomes - New Insights Changes

Summarize What You Have Learned This Week

How Did Meditation, Fasting and Prayer Impact Your Life This Week?

Follow Through:

One of the most important aspect of a fast is the follow through. After the Lord has given you new insight and revelation to your problems or concerns there must be a willingness and a commitment to act and complete the fasting process.

- Think through your strategy.
- How will you implement what you have learned during this week?

Implementation Plan

BIBLIOGRAPHY

Bolesch, D. G. (1988). *The Struggle of Prayer.* Colorado Springs, Helmers & Howard Publishers.

Bounds, E. M. (2006). *The Necessity of Prayer.* Great Britain, Christian Heritage.

Foster, R. J. (1988). *Celebration of Discipline: The Path Spiritual Growth.* San Francisco, Harper & Row.

Foundation, T. H. (1971). *The Living Bible.* Carol Stream, Tyndale House Publishers Inc.

Frances Jane, C. (1820-1915). *I am Thine O Lord {Draw me Near].* New York Brightest and Best.

Hallseby, O. (1994). *Prayer.* Minneapolis, Augsburg Fortress.

Henry, M. *Matthew Henry Complete Commentary on the whole Bible.* from http://www.studylight.org/commentaries/mhm/genesis-5. html. 1706.

Holy Bible: *New Living Translation: NLT.* Carol Stream, Tyndale House Publishers Inc. (2015)

MacArthur, J. (2006). *Alone with God: Rediscovering the Power & Passion of Prayer.* Colorado Springs, Victor.

New American Standard Bible: *(NASB)* La Habra, The Lockman Foundation. (1995)

New King James Version: *The NKJV Study Bible.* Nashville, Thomas Nelson, Inc. (2007).

Nickson, Ann (2002). Bonhoeffer on Freedom: *Courageously Grasping Reality, Ashgate New Critical Thinking in Religion, Theology & Biblical Studies.* Burlington, UK. Ashgate Publishing Company

Park, Andrew Sung. (2004). *From Hurt to Healing. A Theology of the wounded.* Nashville, Abingdon Press.

The ESV Bible: *The Holy Bible, English Standard Version.* Wheaton, Good News Publishers.(2016)

The Living Bible *(LB)* Carol Stream, Tyndale House Publishers Inc. (1971)

The Message *(MSG).* Colorado Springs, NavPress Publishing Group. (2002)

Towns, E. L. (1996). *Fasting For Spiritual Break Through.* Ventura, Regal books.

Underhill, Evelyn. (1985). *The Spiritual Life.* New York, Morehouse Publishing.

Zondervan (2009). *The Holy Bible, New International Version.* Grand Rapids, Zondervan.

NOTES

NOTES